This Is a Land of Wolves Now

Poems by J. Lester Allen

Kung Fu Treachery Press
Rancho Cucamonga, CA

Copyright © J. Lester Allen, 2019
First Edition 1 3 5 7 9 10 8 6 4 2
ISBN: 978-1-950380-14-5
LCCN: 2019935919

Design, edits and layout:
Cover image: J. Lester Allen
Title page image: J. Lester Allen
Author photo: Seth Conley
All rights reserved. No part of this publication may be reproduced or transmitted in any form or by any means, electronic or mechanical, including photocopying, recording or by info retrieval system, without prior written permission from the author.

The author would like to thank the following publications where some of these poems first appeared: *Blacklisted Magazine, Poesy, Decomp, The New York Quarterly, Meat, Red Fez, Up The Staircase, Kill Poet.*

CONTENTS

a cockroach in the penthouse / 1
lost / 3
I've found your broken nowhere / 4
hey sucker, are you lonely? / 7
don't come back from the moon / 10
a lion in the landscape / 13
I would follow James Wright into battle / 15
stand up in the darkness / 17
too dimension / 18
alone amongst a million tiny rockets / 19
the whale with wolves' eyes / 21
dependence day / 23
how not to train a dog / 25
blackbird, she has your eyes / 27
spring / 30
snow days, Socrates and a longing / 32
a street car named get the fuck out / 35
on the good days / 38
how it's done in the dust / 40
love, the first time / 43
termite / 44
thunder mt. / 45
this is a land of wolves now / 46
survival / 48
the wax people / 49
throwing rocks at the sun / 51
the barber / 53

treefingers / 56
a latent dynamo / 58
Martha's (rotten) Vineyard / 60
the calculated sway of perfection / 62
communication breakdown / 63
cabbage patch kid in the mouth of a lion / 64
the cock and the swan / 65
dungeon crawl / 67
rubbernecked / 69
looking for a place to hide when
    the world goes out / 71
Milky Way / 75
no symphony / 78
drowning fishes / 80
closing time / 82
all that poetry is / 84
a beautiful day on Neptune / 85
battleground / 86
a child tied to a roller coaster & hurled
    into outer space / 88
faster than the eye / 89
chance / 91
a deduction of self / 93
action figure / 95
inertia / 96
natural cause / 97
they can't all be Picassos / 100

swarm of nothing / 101

love / 103

Jesus save us all / 104

laying on a Scottish hillside thinking about the masses
and little else besides / 106

by the sea / 109

some get strong and some get strange / 111

success / 113

This Is a Land of Wolves Now

For Christopher Alan Murdoch, in loving memory

a cockroach in the penthouse

there is muted guilt climbing
this ladder of spine;
a lone cockroach
beneath a refrigerator
humming along to the tune
of a stale indifference.

the bad of habit worn
like flower in a young girl's hair
or a path into this brown shag,

how to stop this thing? I ask myself,
while wandering the walls
searching for a switch to
switch or plug to pull,
I feel like Willy
Wonka must have after
one too many elevator rides
trying to give it all away,
but the bellhop won't even
speak to me he just
mumbles into his
lapel like a gagged
man in a gangster's
trunk.
it all matters very little anyway—
this building stands so tall

that the sun is always
setting and God, wherever he is
is continually phoning my room
politely asking for me to leave.
and each time I
answer I tell him
soon soon—
the book deal is all
but signed, the travelling carnival
has an opening for a bowlegged
half-wit who can make failure look like art,
I start next week.
my woman's got a dead uncle
in Tucson who
wants to buy us a
house. we're gonna have
some kids, get some dogs, horses,
eventual divorce and other fatal
failings of heart, I tell him.
and each time he seems to humor me,
there's a level of satisfaction that comes through,
but wouldn't you know it,
much like a telemarketer intent on
selling you aluminum siding and new storm windows
for a house you don't even own,
that old omnipotent, peddler of sunrises and
infomercial eternity
keeps calling
back.

lost

we are all just better parts
and worse
parts
of the same insane
creature,
wandering the earth
in search of
its head

but only ever finding

empty
dusty
skulls.

I've found your broken nowhere

some days the sun and others no
sun only clouds full of rain
and streets for cars
trees for birds, sheds for hammers and
saws, old hidden piles
of *Hustler* magazines

kitchen tables but no dinner, tv but
no entertainment, beds but no sex
or too much sex and
not enough love
houses without husbands or wives
or children and leaky pipes in the
basement
always leaky pipes

windows to peek into or
out from, squirrels to miss
mail boxes to hit
old men who like young men
say *Come on in. I ain't gonna tell nobody.*
I got an extra swimsuit,
let's you and me go sit by the pool.

and sometimes it's the sun or
pretty woman on a catalogue—

purely framed thoughts about
a dirty thing
sometimes it's old ladies
or new ladies or insane old farmers,
workers of the earth
sinners on the hill or preachers in
the trailer park

sometimes this mailman gets a
haircut, sometimes the bridge is
out, sometimes gas is 3 dollars, other
times much more
sometimes the cute attendant there
all prairie-eyed mad
winks at me
she says to me, *You should come around back,*
though I never go, sometimes the
kittens come out, they are curious
end up dead on the road
with rotten-fly-eyes
while the trees
sway in the breeze
other times houses
get painted or become unpainted
as the wallpaper peels I think
of these things, while
officers arrest and lawyers
argue law, the septic man pumps sludge
of man never-ending

the one true product of
our existence
while kids swing swings,
bat balls, catch grasshoppers or
caterpillars or other things

burn the world down.

mowed lawns mean nothing
well-furnished homes mean
nothing

not much holds any meaning
men live for money and die for it
too
not much ever changes
in our tiny little lives
we see only what
we want to see,
believe true only what we
can control,

and explaining away the rest

everything is right in
the world except everything that
isn't—
everywhere.

hey sucker, are you lonely?

there's a chrome horse in
the front street
the leaves there made mad
with blowing

I've consumed enough
Pabst
to kill all but the staunchest
of my cells

Molina coming thru
the speakers
reminding me that
it's ok to
want to piss it all away
feeling the absence of love,
and understanding and
a guilt too much,
like rhododendrons opening
in the rain.

I went to a used
book sale
earlier and scored
18 of the greats for under

4 bucks and
met a polygamist in
plaid socks
who wondered what my afternoon
was looking like.

I was almost interested too
until she explained what
a communication logjam
the whole thing was and
how each partner needed to be sure that
all others were happy
with their situations.
I made up something about
a train and
my needing to be on it,
she still somehow managed
my number.

this one time I ate a cactus
that I purchased on
eBay
and thought I saw God
but I didn't see God
and now it's raining again
buckets of phony
thoughts.

I get up,
decide to eat,
smash my head on the corner of the cupboard,
am down for 15 minutes
and when
I come to;
the food is on fire

and
the phone rings,

but it's the wrong woman.

don't come back from the moon

breakfast on a green park bench in
early March
while eating a fast
food hash brown I think of
your bones
cracking from the weight of flight
and helicoptering like
sycamore seeds
back against the earth.

we have harnessed the power of gods
fashioned the means to explore other
worlds with the speed of a thousand
cheetahs but instead, box ourselves in,
it is our nature to be lazy,
unimaginative, sometimes even unbearable—
sweaty, gluttonous paper giants we,
asleep on the crushed dreams of
a fawn while amassing such great wealth
with the ease of a falcon's wings in flight
and encased in ego and a misunderstanding
of the way of things so everywhere
that even the sun, even the
waitresses and the
squirrels, mutt dogs and purebred

politicians will bark at you,
shake their tails at you,
inform you that they are out of Tabasco,
highlight your insignificance, give birth to
a shadow, tell you
untruths, whatever they need to do
to be free of you,

as we collectively walk the dirt unknowingly
photographing the trees
unknowingly, passing an air between our lips
that will never quite belong to us
but it does belong to this magnificent
holy shit of a rock whose greatest threat
walks and talks
and texts and
does not look where it
is going in a supermarket isle
with hands full of avocados,
laughs and births
and kills,
shits, cries,
takes selfies,
watches *Survivor* reruns,
reads (and writes) this book, plays the
stock market
and thinks itself collectively
intelligent, reaps and reaps
and reaps, never stopping to listen

to the blood of
itself or
remembering that one time
we put a ghost
on the moon.

a lion in the landscape

we were in Philadelphia, at a museum
it was many of the works of Dali.
3 and 3 quarter hours of madness; and when we left,
the air no longer looked right. and the people walked up and
down the sides of the street in the rain, but they hardly looked
 right either.
and I thought of this time, as a child
when I melted many crayons on top of my father's wood stove,
 waiting
for my canvas to cool before crafting my masterpiece.
he beat my ass good for that one
(it was deserved.)
and I thought then, and still think now—
how is a man supposed to create when he can't set his mind
 without some hand
waiving out from the darkness to restore order?
some voice of pale-reason like cyclone, like flame on
the edges of a
moment.
and you've got it there, right between your ears
like a confused rat in a
cage only in those last few seconds
it finds the faulty latch and freedom.
I remember reading somewhere that Dali would
host large orgies but couldn't bring himself to
participate,

or it wouldn't work or
couldn't work and he sat there instead as a boy
at an ice cream buffet with no tongue might.
it's harder than it looks, getting the mind right,
whether sex or art
fingering the gun,
setting your sights.. breathing, breathing,
breathing and then no breathing..
POP
as the fingers relax, you set down the rifle
   and quietly disappear
once more into the crowd.

I would follow James Wright into battle

this poem is a dream
inside a war and the
meaning is a wolfsbane tea of
things; a nail in a worn shoe soul realized too late
or man whistling *When the Saint's go Marching In*
in a public restroom, just the two
of you standing there, returning what has
been borrowed— and he won't stop
and Christ, why won't he stop? and at that moment
    I beg of something
unseen for a storm to come and for it
to blow everything back to sea but people in situations like mine
are rarely so lucky,
knowing this, I side-saddle the awkward horse
of myself and ride out, encumbered with the thought of an
uninterrupted, everywhere happiness and not understanding
    it (that, and a great many other things)
but if you can believe it (and I bet that you can) it
goes on in the tiniest parts of
everything; a secret, silent sugar turned
septic wound, let go for too long
and the doctor says simply that
they must take the leg and
they send the poor guy home, back to someplace like
    Scottsbluff, Nebraska and

his father's pig farm. it wasn't *his* war anyway,
I think and now gathering 'round our makeshift barracks
in a exceedingly soggy, exceedingly golden
field, down one but still
a few million strong,
in ragged war fatigues
with a sprig of hollyhocks pinned
to each one of our chests like medals of
being, we take up arms in the name
of what each has lost, or never had
to lose and roll forth
as some great steam roller
of a lenient desire
thundering across this impossible
mountain,

a soft-eyed legion in
the rain.

stand up in the darkness
(for Kate)

no feral, mad morning here
no accredited sun to chase off and
away, down a rickety flame escape
to the broke-bottled streets below.
no breakfast tales over last night's
left over sake of riding all night in a truck full of dynamite
across some empty-desert-holiday-lone-man-wandering-
love-song-soon-yet-still-not-yet-written-road.
I've found love in this desert, amidst the bones of other
dead things. other lost and raw, skin-prick-rash, hack-
sawed, busted and beautiful things.
Lomachenko on last evening's TV and not but some odd
blocks away punching his way to victory and immortality,
with the footwork of a laser guided ballet dancer carefully
moving his way through fire.
they say James Dean once lived here for two of his brief 24
years and I've found love in these crisp white unlonely bed
sheets that once covered the many ghosts of a fear-dream
procession.
there's a day out there
and feet for walking;
rising to twist the blinds away
the darkness goes. at the foot of
the bed I bend to kiss the toes
of an unfamiliar kind of day.

too dimension

ever is the bastard
son, beaten down and dusted of
all pride-things
knows nothing of dreams
but the rein of
humiliation.

I'm sorry, said the waving bush
to the ground,
but it really is not nearly as
much fun as it
seems.

a white car descends
a far-off mountain
carrying three clean smiles
and as many diseased
appendices.

somewhere,
under the ribs
there, like a hand in
the dark,
friend.

there,
we got you.

alone amongst a million tiny rockets
(to the New Year, happy or not)

and rarely is the timing right, sitting
in a college-town bar
surrounded by people half my age
alone in a coat on permanent loan
keys to car lost somewhere
out in the snow,
dignity, perhaps not far off.
I can sense the drafty grin of my 38 years
widening
but the feeling is lost on me.

ineptitude clings
tightly
to the brain like a kid sister during a scary movie
in a crowded theater,
as I drink at my beer the
oceans turn their heads away.
the pursuit of happiness has ground
the gears of many, I take a wet thumb
and press it into my
own failures
revealing only the mirror beneath.
I shake off the reality and figure I've got enough fire in me
to take on a few of these youth-fooled blowhard types,

who may or may not be shooting beams of disdain in my
direction, but instead somehow manage to
ignore the escalating conversation between the beer and
tequila in my gut.
I get up, walk away from the snowflakes
and into the snowstorm—
still no sign of
keys, dignity...
I hunch beneath a stone wall,
soul calling out to the ink-well darkness—

somewhere it's a peach
a mossbunker
a ball
a sardine or
opossum in a cage

a red rose

a pink one

or no damn thing at all.

the whale with wolves' eyes

while lifting Garcia Lorca's words
off
the silken page
the machines of men grew
silent
my throat like caged dog,
chest flocked by
harlequin doves
the whales all had wolves' eyes,
by God!
the platypus in heat bayed
like a hound
in hunt.

my eye,
the right one
twitched uncontrollably,
like a hummingbird
on methamphetamine
like a fly
spotted by
cat and forever derided
by a subtle lack
of everything,
I flipped page after page—

unable to think about
anything else

(neither mouse nor man)

for quite sometime
after.

and much as a moon
grown tired and
broken apart
from itself,
much as a dinner plate
shattered on
a cold January floor,
the lawn-chair lives
of other men

—*with subtle squeaking*—
folded ever so nervously in
upon
themselves.

dependence day
(for J. Dorsey)

*you can be anything that
   you want to be* she said
   if you'd only put your mind to it.
I want to be a ferryman on
   the river of Styx, I replied
  working the split
        shift with Charon.
maybe then   I could finally
    understand   why people
         cry at funerals
why old ladies cling to
     their copies of
Harper's Bazaar like
oxygen tanks for
   emphysema or what
death's touch might truly
     feel like
and all the guts
inside Fort Mc Henry wouldn't get
Washington across this river any
quicker than a flash of his wooden
       smile   with Molly Pitcher
      there   dressing
        wounds

                for a Mr. America
                    pageant   now she had
            style   too bad she couldn't
                be here to open my
        head and inspect the
    contents before swapping them
                out for replacement
    maybe then I could
    write an Independence
    Day poem that would
    make our forefathers
                proud   but my heart
    is just too involved to
            have me believe that
    there isn't some truth
    to the saying   that nothing in this
                life is free and in looking around
            I'd have to say that
                    Francis Scott Key mustn't have been much
                            of a writer

how not to train a dog

I once knew a lonely woman
who lived
just down the road

she told all of her ex husbands once
that obedience was a
necessary evil

I think of a Schnauzer at such times
and how a man
in the eyes of his master would be forced to act like
something else,
anything else
in the name of survival—
the poor hound
could have the blood cooked right out of his being
just for being,
4 hours of freedom on a Sunday,
don't say a word
or show your teeth to the crowd..
these people want it soft,
hollow,
deboned, debunked

do not get excited about the color
of the weather

after all, it is not the color of
your neighbor's skin.

like a loyalist's lost
Instagram photos
snapping pictures of award-winning
posture,
it would appear
that being a one trick pony
in a three-
ring circus
is little more
than poor
arithmetic

but what do I know?
I still refuse to believe
that obedience
is not one
of the seven deadly sins

and will, on occasion
shit behind the couch
when no one is looking.

blackbird, she has your eyes

she sits by the window
eating an orange
while the juice dribbles
down
her
chin.

she hides a knife from me
in her shoe,
an entire army beneath her tongue
waiting to invade.

she is very clever, this one.

I went somewhere else with my eyes
when she got it out
and stuck it in,
parading the dead parts of me
through the streets,
shaming my troops,
beheading my generals,

even impaling my minister of
foreign relations.

sometimes a man thinks that he has it all figured,
neatly laid out.
assuming a sock to be a sock,
that stripes are stripes and that
jeans will never go out of style.

how wrong we are.

and when it is these things that prove themselves
untrue, it becomes
everything.

smiles & gas gauges,
dates on milk cartons,
good news, bad news, no news,
a poignant truth masquerading behind the face of
contentment
and all of it like wiping your ass with
wax paper.

and that dumbfounded look about your face
when you come to find that the greeting card
companies never devised a category for
this kind of love,
well, it's that very idea that keeps us fighting
our way
back to the bar
for one more drink,

for one last gaze at those high-heeled
dream stilts
carrying the good of our lives away

while we suck at the discomposing air
and think
at first about nothing and then
maybe,
about the upcoming baseball season
about engines and a well-lubed
bedlam in the streets of
a somewhere city
that's any city
but the one currently hovering over you
with a foot planted firmly in your chest,
supplying constant reminder
of the one that got away.

believe me, you sure can learn a lot
by watching somebody suck the life
from an orange.

tip that drink
and wait patiently
for the next one.

spring

you glorious miracle.
have warmed the frost,

have painted the gray
&
assuaged the mind.

from overhead
somewhere,
a meadowlark
calls.

it is almost
hot
at 72 degrees.

I think of Africa
where 72 degrees is not
at all
hot.

to my left,
the cat crouches
like a leopard
in the brush,

while
quietly,
the mind
elephants
away.

snow days, Socrates and a longing

I'm stuck in
snowing for 8 days and nights and
the car won't go up the hill, 8 days of
waiting for love and the postman
and the pipes are frozen solid.
I stand over a pot of boiling water in the kitchen
dragging a grout sponge over the dirtier parts
of myself— 8 long days of naked waiting,
drinking Irish cream from the bottle and playing cards with
a large blue ermine when I at once sink beneath
the floorboards and miraculously
it's spring and I'm at the Kentucky Derby and
everwhere people and
people and people, horses
horses, then more people
again.

Paul Newman is there, Socrates and the Marquis De Sade,
and my woman, looking good dressed in
a sliver of tailored sunset and hot pink heels
approaches the table where we are sitting (all take notice)
and takes a seat between me and
the Marquis just as Mr. Newman starts up about
racing, 4-legged, 4-wheeled, drag coefficients and
tire compositions and all
so cool so cool.
I kept thinking, this guy could convince a legion

of pacifists to take up arms
in revolt against the government if
they'd only quit getting lost in
his gaze.
Socrates sits to his left silently
save for several groans of
various lengths and tones
he briefly nods when Paul begins talking about the
essence of a race, the white-knuckled, calibrated bravado
of it all,
and as he does the sauce from his recently consumed Reuben
drips from his moustache to
his beard,
he looked a bit confused throughout the
entire process, if I'm being honest though
I must say, the guy rocks a 3-piece seersucker as well as
any man I've ever seen.
Newman has shifted gears and is now commenting on the state of
the country when the Marquis remarks that he thinks
Paul would make a wonderful president
to which he somewhat coyly replies that his acting talents
might find him overqualified for the position.
I turn to see the Marquis' reaction but he and
my woman had suddenly vanished
into the crowd.
I excuse myself, grabbing a handful of pistachios as I
depart
in search of spectacle and scandal,
making my way to the concourse I watch a centaur in a sun dress
rearrange the clouds, I'm not sure when but the whole
thing somehow became a movie only now I'm an extra

without any lines as I walk from camera to camera
trying to appear unbothered
about what had happened with my lady and
the Marquis except I'm not wearing any shoes and
my pockets are full of sandwich swords and
a realized heartache,
and just then some drunken fool runs into me
spilling his drink all over my bad time and I punch him
square in the mug just to see what will happen,
he crumbles much more easily
than anticipated and as he does the crowd suddenly starts
going wild, screaming, hollering mad
COME ON BLUEBALLS! someone from behind me yells.
YEEEEEEEAAH BABY, THE FOUR IS GONNA DO IT!
another screams.
I look up as the majestic gray colt blazes past the finish
there were no other horses
anywhere,
Blueballs stood there in the winner's area
and there, having ridden him to victory
was my friend
Mr. Newman,
they gave the horse some flowers,
they gave Paul some flowers,
he smiled and the crowd cheered
some more.

a streetcar named get the fuck out

It came off the page thrashing cayenne mad as
a rhino in a tenement hall, like something T. Williams
might have penned while shambling through the wine-soaked
madness of his twilight.
I played the lead in a feverish pantomime (reviews were sub-
optimal) dancing on a hot tin roof that went on for miles
and years in either direction, and when we buried the puppy
in the yard next to the shed in the rain on that Christmas Eve.
morning I figured the worst had to be behind us
or at least
beneath, but its odd how these things go
when you've got no buoy of hope to look to;
no guide to lead you worn and
defeated up Mt. Venus &
the mongrel dog,
the beast is always waiting..
and while walking strange city blocks after the bomb
I found myself at a bar, a mostly black establishment
save for myself, and though penniless was I
those good-natured souls bought me beer
after beer and
a man named Mingo, the bar owner/ pimp/
Jolly Saint Nick that he was
paraded his women out giving me my choice,
Gonna have to pass Mingo, I told him,
My woman, immortal beauty that she is would never forgive it.

I thanked the gang, when as I left
a car from somewhere followed me
down the empty street and into the alleyway,
backed in I managed myself
atop a dumpster and over a large wall
when my feet hit the ground the last of my sobriety
was puked out all over that alley and ready was I
to hand my self over to the cold isolation
but soon after a squad car pulled up, *you okay?* it asked.

I told it, *I'm not from around here, visiting my woman's family, think I'm lost.*
Small town that it was the officer knew my hosts
and offered a ride.
Wasn't the warmest of welcomes when the car pulled in to the drive
but I managed inside, as the parties warred over
whether or not to return me to the night,
then the ruling was handed down and I was exiled to the couch, which is where
I found myself the next morning
sipping at an awkward coffee, when out of nowhere and without warning of any kind
the tree came crashing down—
all lights and wet, shattered glass of a mess
that it was,
I jumped up, threw my hands in the air
feeling the need to proclaim my innocence

as everyone rushed into the room
and collectively stood there for a minute

staring on in disbelief

as if Kris Kringle himself had just terminated out
right there on the living room floor,

then all at once we set about picking up the mess of
toppled tree and broken heirloom ornaments,
used-up hookers, polite police boys
and dead puppies—

that was one hell of a Christmas.

on the good days

I eat sunshine
spit the seeds into the
gutters
devour the blocks in shoes
not made for heavy walking

I smile when the dogs bark at
me, disproving my belief that
I am no longer here

whenever the women bark
(it is rare)
I smile even louder
pull *threads of awareness*
from my shirt
draw imaginary doors
in the sky

walk thru them and disappear

life is a thrift store that I
am inside of
browsing the shirts, pants,
bald heads of mannequins
with chips in their synthetic
flesh,

meat grinders,
stereos with one speaker
and a broken tape deck
suits with no
bottoms
pots with no
tops

dust
dust
dust
old paperbacks and
the many shoes of the dead

I purchase nothing
it is good to abstain sometimes
it is better to be hungry,
lonely, sober and
wanting

it keeps a man moving forward

I step back into the street
grabbing at the sound of passing cars
with both fists
and trying not
to let go.

how it's done in the dust
(for S. Conley)

about 2 hrs outside of Las Cruces at the station,
2 hrs of driving, two years of driving—
hauling gear from stage to stage in a
land that looked like it was drawn
by Mel Blanc were he
an impressionist on ayahuasca—
all road-runner rockiness and
mesas for miles,
dust just biding its time
before the great reclamation
of everything,
and now my hands hurt
and the gas won't pump fast
enough and there's something
in my eye, sand or a festering perspective—
things I've seen that can't ever be unseen
and just then I looked over my shoulder
and there, through the waves of
heat and arid malaise
I saw a man coming down the hill
crisp white painter's overalls, face wearing a cigarette and
everywhere stare,
like a caged feral dog,
and the gasoline wouldn't pump fast
enough and as he got

closer I saw some thing strapped to his chest,
long, mechanical and I thought
about the station attendant
and how she'd managed along
in this dry baked hell of a place
and if she'd ever get out
or even wanted to get out
and still the man got closer
face covered in grime
as he walked up to
a different pump
much less white and crisp and
started filling
started filling his mechanical
death dealer
of a thing and still
the gas would not pump
goddamnit
and he pulled the cord
and like some weed eradicating Excalibur
it roared to life as he stood there and then began
whipping the thing into the air
like he was swatting invisible flies the
size of pterodactyls; I figured it likely he
was the scout of some end times army
and soon the rest would be coming down over the hill
to rape and pillage and swallow
everything

and I thought about
trying to save the attendant
but it was too late for her anyway
and I jumped back in the van and sped away
the crazy maniacal sonofabitch
dancing on forever
in the rear-view.

love, the first time

I stood in the sun,
kept taking my hands
in and out of
my pockets.
I saw you but
pretended not to.
you chewed gum
and kicked your heels, gently.

that's one lucky bench, I thought.

I saw a very reasonable
blue tree
and climbed it
three times,

your name
never leaving
my mouth.

termite

she,
the best of her
makes like glue

also,
her shattered voice
says—
July is a friend
of uncertain
emotion

the cat curls
around feet
at the head
of a table

that
the walls fall down
around.

thunder mt.

if ever not
found to be
pleasing
your mouth will conceal,
like an ancient color code of
berries,

this space.

that
a thunder fills,
but no amount of
rain
is
ever gonna
wash away.

this is a land of wolves now

I see a small child crying
in a stroller as its
mother pushes it across the uneven
cracks of the social economic fault
line and
away and I think
that I am satisfied when the
fog comes to this place
and covers over
the unsightly things:
rotting bones of far-off
industry,
corporate rabbit-fuck monopoly,
salaciously veneered behind a
demagogue's smile,
bull-shit religious synergy
cock-mucking child-fuckers holing
down in a house of the holy

everything is the same

people lured into repetition
by repetition—
the salt-lick sadness of the unattainable
dream

waiting for our own shadow to
cut ahead of us in line as they
chant something about
freedom from their oppressors
only to realize that in the end
we're all angry wolves in
people clothing.

God loves, albeit
inappropriately, and man
it seems, is just here to
kill.
don't believe me?
walk the halls of any
Ivy League university
watch Maury Povich while discussing Proust
with a Russian girl
in your underwear
on the phone.
mow the lawn while trying
not to think about the neighbor's
young daughter
sunbathing
a first down or two
away or
the worst thing imaginable
that you would do
at any given moment
for love.

survival

drown your cellphone in the sink,
barricade the door,

eat peaches from
a can.
marvel at cats &
mice & starlings,
keep your fingers out
of car doors and do not cook your meat
too thoroughly.

keep a good book in every
room of your house
and set your dreams
a sail
down a river of lost love.

if you can manage
to get along
without them,
you'll
be
fine.

the wax people

to find pause

just long enough
in this distilled
existence
some dry-rehearsed rock opera that
the spiders can
tap in their webs and upon
my brain

this has been the way,
the best kept secret of
my survival

I wait with the crickets
for a something come shovel the dust
from the damp corners of my mind
a sweet voice that
I'd do best forgetting
while passing time, waiting upon
this old sickness
like worms for rain
while the far away sun hides a jealousy with
proper poker face and
the wax people, they grow old
but never seem to

age while wishing for hearts
for brains
for hernias,
a sweet salty flesh to caress or
curtain the thought
of bone,
a lasting credibility
and yet,
still some time on the clock
one more season of wheedled believing
while planes go up & down
& buildings
& moods
& lives
and those of us still here
writing about it
complaining about it
& suffering from it,
we are all quietly
and some of us not so quietly
left wishing
for the same.

throwing rocks at the sun (repeat, repeat)

that feeling, of being sometimes the dirt
or pot but rarely the flower. a wilting realist in a
you've got to be fucking kidding world
with nowhere to tie horse.

I am renewed slightly by the pale glow of the unknown,
crawling towards the light with three good knees and a less
than stellar perception of things, and much like Sartre
sitting amongst old
French furniture,
I do desperately want out.

everything smells of an empty arena after a split-decision
title fight
or used shell casings in a pile on the front lawn,
a pyrrhic scent, neither victory nor defeat with enough intrigue
only to keep the feet shuffling on ahead,
it's $20 an hour for a lifetime and yet
no balance in the morality bank, with good sense all dried up
like mice eyes in an oven.
it's 28 years of sadness running towards you with pants put on
one leg at a time
and bayonets
fixed—
the inability to cry at the bad movie of life.
an un-mendable mood with

no porcelain toes to kiss
and no thoughts of pardon.
when it comes I want it to be like the ash of a good cigar
falling at the master's feet,
like a 5 alarm fire,
like the glint in the eyes of an unborn child—
choking on the
funicular ironies,
while desperately screaming
just
to be.

the barber

to awake alone
on your own couch
much too small and with no other sound option
for sleep, a railroad crick of agony
scaling the length of your spine,
it is almost noon
and hungover with an eternal disappointment
I lay here now,
bits of sun coming in
thru dirty windows and
unwashed mop of hair have I
which gets me thinking
Sunday weird kinds of thoughts
about cleaning up
my act and getting a hair cut
making myself *presentable* as they say
and thinking of the last person
entrusted
besides myself, to take steel to this mess
in the last 16 years,
some shit-crazy barber
always laughing like an 18-wheels coming down
a mountain without brakes
and passing stories thru a burnt out
salesman's smile.

he always had new cars and
dirty jokes that I didn't understand
and much advice on women
that I could never remember.
I do remember the day
when they wrestled the braces
from my teeth and I circled the block
and walked in and Big Ed,
seeing that it was a special day,
cut my hair for free.
I was 14 then and it was the first time
that I ever saw a bit of decency
creep out from within his
tired, flabby body
and not too long after that
staring at the television
one night
and there was Big Ed's face
on the screen.
police lights and paramedics were accompanying
a black body bag wheeled out of a house
on a gurney.

turns out ol' Ed had been busying himself
with much more than perfecting the crew cut.
the law found his business partner
shot in the head,
deader than a bird run out of sky

then Ed led police on a cross-state chase
that ended in Tennessee
where he held his estranged
wife and
daughter hostage
with a gun.
but ol' Ed, fidgety, cantankerous sort that he was
must have grown tired of that
and with the fuzz closing in
he turned the cannon
upon himself.

I still think about him
now and again
and the hockey sticks that used to hang
from the walls of his shop
signed by every member
of the championship team and every time
the thoughts of him
come pulsing across the wires
of my brain
I find myself getting quiet
and am glad that I never understood his jokes,
or took any of his advice
on women.

treefingers

working at my brain
over cold coffee and
pie

if in a hundred attempts
something
fails in
ninety-eight of them then
it is time for
something else,

time to put that dog down
with one between the eyes
time to clear the
pieces
from the chess
board

and begin again.

I am scuba gear
in the middle of a
desert,

a
bottom-

less
pail,

cookie cutters in shapes
that your mother
wouldn't approve
of.

I am standing
now,

staring out the window
at the silver side of a December rose
bush.

it's Christmas morning
and much like the empty
bed with pillows and blankets
all to myself,

this house
feels
strangely
comfortable

without you
in it.

a latent dynamo

pressed magnolias make rain,
my past is a grounded eagle searching peace
with the ratios of love and indifference
clutching old post cards of street-scapes in
                                  Warsaw
  the mice come out of the walls,
  the mice come out of the walls,
the cats would rather wait the handout line
than earn a keep here.

I place a call to my mechanic,
says the brakes are shot- line and pad and
caliper, will be another week or more before it is ready.
It's January 8th, I cannot find the sun or reason to
get out of bed, though the morning's coffee and
last night's chili will soon provide one. There's a sound of
distant wood on chopping block and true hands with axe of
the centuries carrying forth fire and wheel, language and
medicine, machine guns, televisions, space-travel and
                Snapchat.
the internet is down, again. I feel a large rock in the middle
of a river as icy water of information flows all
around me. I am dry with knowing though feel with certainty
the government is still at standstill, with droning chatter over
    walls and
    birthrights—

words from grown fools like wheat in the fields
of forgetting,
a soft-shelled disillusionment swells in a blue-collar
marrow of recalcitrance and while all of this,
a familiar voice says to my eagle,

eagle, your eyes may carry you away
as swift as an arrow willed in flight, as a kite string tied to
a belly of wind,
but your infirm wings and soft teeth,
  ever-obedient thumbs and crux of reason
will see you full of doubt before you ever find the sky.

I glance at the majestic creature, enamored with
his reflection in the window, breaking pose only
to chase an itch through his feathers.
I shake my head, get out of bed, a
second cup of coffee, sit down and fiddle with
a broken watch on the nightstand.

my eagle, notorious hustler,
juggernaut of
achievement, prolific
champion of success,

tomorrow..

Martha's (rotten) Vineyard

two sweating,
heaving
fish on sandy beach
a labored love like
breathing of some almost
dead thing
the voice on the phone
of ex-wife, still married but each with our own state
of mind,
jealousy and 20 dollar clam chowder makes me
the asshole that I am today, and though
ultimately, I do not really care how many of Han Solo's sons
you've fucked
there is an inescapable truth of fist,
of claw
and maybe I am punching above weight
of a factory man's son, and maybe the girl you caught me
with the evening after was
only nineteen.
though you did cut me open and leave me for the gulls,
perhaps that first one that split my lip only really drew
perspective,
it's possible that your heart simply isn't near as pretty
as the rest of you,
I've considered the possibility while serving my sentence

on this undeniable prison, giving in, giving way
I wander this island at night- knives out
see a lonely starfish below streetlight
crying into her cellphone,
throw my shoes in the ocean,
phone the Office of Domestic Affairs
and while on hold and listening to the Muzak version
of *Love Hurts*
I realize that this island is too damn small to ever serve as
venue for our title fight
and has the loneliest
lighthouses that I've
ever seen.

the calculated sway of perfection

the fondling of existence
    in the hunt
  for answers to
      the eternal
         dilemma—
    the terms
  the lunacy
     the inconsequence of
   contempt.

the tie drawn tight
   around the neck
of the blood-line
 as it dangles
    from the rafters—

success smiling
behind one
    of its many masks.

communication breakdown

birds of summer
gone crickets &
frogs moths dance
for porch light love

you said it she said
YOU said it I said

& nothing is ever said
which isn't somehow
                              true

the garage gets so
     depressed in the
              winter.

cabbage patch kid in the mouth of a lion

crawling the cave of
yourself
pitiful hands
and bruised knees,
stomach,
soul

looking up at the sparrow
in the trees
and wondering:

how did you get
so high?

the cock and the swan

it is a pair of shoes
tucked in an
inappropriate corner or
forgetting to buy lunch meat
at the grocery store
it is a road trip with
poor directions or
none at all
careless syllables slipping
off the lips that
aren't readily retrieved

it's all the tiny little things
that make up
the big thing
the mystery we live
but never bother trying
to solve

like a drunk dinner
conversation at
your parent's
place that goes
nowhere
and ends in
God

like me standing
in the doorway
talking to tigers
from a distant
planet
in the universe
that is
your
mind

doing that
then quietly
shutting the door
behind me.

dungeon crawl

i bathe my thoughts in
the stomachs of frogs
happy to have your smile
the bright wind cannot touch me
the fly
i am ice cream cool in
the many eyes of Christ

it is the same for all of us
i'd imagine—
   we find our voices in the
            rings of trees
in reflections of ancient
armor while searching carefully
for point of entry with
one thrust
through flesh
   and bone
then finally the victory of blood the
sound of joints
resigning
as the beast collapses at your feet
twitching just a little and
then still

at this point two words of advice;
expose only enough weakness
to lure them in and never
lower your sword—

with any luck at all
they will never
quit coming.

rubbernecked

the words
clean and pure like
unwed mothers or leather belt
across the back
ship sailing blindly towards
shore
the cat kills crickets as if
he's Hitler while
Liechtenstein sits quietly on
the couch hammering beers
happy that this poem is beyond   reach

drove the scene of a car crash
tonight in which undoubtedly
everyone had expired and
in the twists of metal and shimmering
reflections of divorced glass
the mind begun searching for the
words, the poem
but a crash like that— all blood and
violence while spinning the dials
of radio or mind
there is no poem
only death arriving like
a childhood memory across the

brain and seeping slowly
into the black pavement below—
the lighthouse gone dark
captain gone mad as the sea
wavesANDwavesANDwaves
to a merciless conglomerate
                        of stars.

looking for a place to hide when the world goes out
(for B. Harney)

the threat of fire or
flood means very little
while resting quite soundly
in a midtown Manhattan hotel room
with clean drapes and
saucer of mints on the dresser
by the door
a room that for a night
has proven feasible but a week
of this could never last so one must stretch
each glorious second like the political
honesty of any politician
working the levers and
flicking that bean
beneath the skirt of
Great Lady Freedom

the lizards slither from the
swamps only to return
as men mean,
unfit and ugly and so disconnected
from life that it isn't even a life

anyone with dirt beneath fingernails and credit card
debt would recognize, but instead
a side-show act at carnival packed
in a railcar next to Hottentot Venus and the Elephant man,
riding the rails to nowhere
and fast

I become curious about the inner workings
of the television and fail to understand
how they manage to cram so many assholes
inside of it—
people who know everything
what a curse, and I do
not wish to cross paths with these
types but as of yet have
found no way to avoid them
in restaurants they will be there
in the museums the
art galleries
the parks
especially in the municipal buildings,
universities
& country clubs
they will be there
thicker than all the other places
like a sap between fingers
trying to make peace
with the whole
only there is never any lasting peace
save the temporary tolerances
of lesser men

striving to be somebody,
anybody and most often times
failing— money cannot make them
nor woman
or lack of golf strokes
or lack of humanity

heads become lodged in assholes
every day and yet
the broken tv mentions nothing of it
it's the next great epidemic,
it's as old as time
and the tv can't be bothered
with what is actual,

the big game is rigged
the news fashioned out of a
top heavy agenda and
old Apple computer parts,

the polar ice caps will
be gone by 2050
the cities of New York
and Los Angeles will be
completely underwater
the atmosphere will become
so poisonous
that even the tiniest of insects
will not be immune
men will turn on each other

for food
for ammunition,
for less than you think
packs of wild dogs
will rule the wilderness
people will forget
how to smile.

after thoughts like these
a hangnail seems most manageable,
a hemorrhoid,
the conditioned air here reminds
me of easier times, the song
of raindrops on the fire escape
railing provides a calmness
not easily bested by modern medicine
or perhaps the good time truly
lies in the simple satisfaction of
knowing that
when the waters do
rise and the flames fix
to blaze
they will be taking
   nothing
                            away
from   me.

Milky Way

that moment when we first
come to understand that we are only each
a tiny little speck of nothing much,
no more than a beetle
on a pile of shit
or the deepest thoughts of a fly,
it is then that the living is
able to begin—
looking at sunsets and
seeing sunsets,
taking refuge from the world
in a cold shower,
cold beer
kicking your high-horse in the balls
and taking your place amongst
the rank and file.

I will readily admit
a fair bit of failure in
these matters
and that it has taken me
some years of undoing
to achieve this calloused
state.

I can remember *exactly*
the time when I first set
upon this change—
while working the night shift
packing candy into boxes,
first making the boxes, taping them
filling them with tray after tray,
wrapping them,
stacking them
over and over and over
and slowly being consumed by the monotony
of it all, when I thought of the planets
and stars out there wrapped up in all
that black
and all the sad, slouch-backed slugs
like myself
working the candy factories of
other worlds
and how meaningless it all was
and how I would
never place importance
upon who I was
or my place amongst men
ever again.

it had this feeling of warmth,
like hot coals in the middle
of my chest, like a hive full of bees busy

making it
and I no longer feared
any of the things we are taught to fear,
and money—
too much or not enough
or even the eventual rotting and disease
of myself.

the candy kept being
pumped out
and I continued boxing
it away, much like a machine
only not thinking oil and
metal parts but instead of 7am
and smiling like a fox
run free from a hen house
in the morning rain
and once outside there
beyond the whirring machines
and sterile fluorescence of industry
was life, and the weather
death, rent and taxes
and a new found ability to keep
moving through it
all.

no symphony

remembering days when we
planted a line of spruce trees to
keep the world away,
said incendiary things—
poison in the ear,
tongues of fire
the lions of those days
toed a careful line—
mercurial mercenaries
that they were, soothed only
by the occasional
calm of a
quiet lie

as I would be hard inside of you
the bees danced in the
late afternoon air.

the blood is redder now,
the kidneys walk hand in hand,
a saunter of knowing—
old champions, bruised and beaten
down
by the world
and in looking for a landfill

to toss the decades away in
I hold a certain hope—
that these bricks might somehow
breathe again,
but even now when you smile
your lips appear to me as if
in black and white;
an old photo of joy
hidden beneath socks in a drawer, as
happiness bends away from my fingers
a broken song.

and my dear,
much like a piano before untrained
fingers I would surely
ruin you in much the
same way that
(in the hands of others)
so much beauty
has been made.

drowning fishes

voices blaring out from the darkness like
rusty trumpets,
all out of money,
all out of booze
then back in the night air
with the rain
howling bastard-moon-coyotes in
some back alley oasis
of a whiskey-tuned mind.
we pulled up hoodies,
put our heads inside as
the bar and the street
and all the other streets
slowly faded away down
over the hill and
conversation shifted
to other things:
good books and
bad movies,
the many recent failures of Tim Burton
specifically, then
women,
and sailing the south pacific on
a dime though
preparing really for nothing spectacular
just then a girl walked by with
beautiful eyes,

bright wet eyes that spoke
like the moon and at that very
moment I felt
like a handsome blue fish
in the hands of
a small child,
the hook still in me
as it rained & rained
and I smiled at words like
Istanbul &
metallurgy
while thinking of the back
seat of my father's car where
a girl first let me get my fingers
inside,
a first love like birdbath
full of feathered promises
and bird shit.
we were together all that school year
and the following summer,
then while on vacation she met some guy-
a cousin of a friend of a friend
and they made it while I was
home and very much not
making it, or anything at all
which is really the long way of saying
that I got screwed
but not in the way that I
wanted to.

closing time
(for T. Scott)

I can still make out the tune
of Pat Boone on the radio
doing Metallica, with a glass of JB
the nearest exit in case things got too wild.
she was a lawyer there on her balcony
and other places too, I'd imagine
and my friend had his tongue in her mouth
just moments before,
he'd say later that she was a terrible kisser
and that moments after their twining of tongues
and hours before he told me about it
he set down his drink and filtered his vomit through the
ivy that clung to the balustrade
of her balcony
and I went inside,
Jim and I being already quite good friends
and I feeling pretty good of things
(he always encouraged me to be at my best)
decided that, in addition to taking a piss in this strange
lawyer's bathroom
that what I really wanted to do was to take
a nice hot bath.
so I drew the water, stripped
down and slipped in
finished the Beam

while I thumbed some pages of Heller's
Closing Time
and thinking about the girl that I'd just met
a few hours ago
in the bar downstairs
while the bartender poured drinks and
slid pieces around a backgammon board
and some of the regulars went
on about the Yankees,
she was making eyes with me
and talking about making wine
and I was talking to her about making poetry.
it was all very wonderful and I thought:
this one could make me forget all the women
that have ever wronged me, and still this might be true
but then her friend got sick
and she had to leave.

the water was getting cold. I shook myself awake
and let it whirl away.
back outside again with my friend, the lawyer, Pat and Jim,
they, too drunk to notice my wet head, offered me more
to drink.
I filled up, then excused myself from the balcony
much as before and stumbled back inside
where I found a large orange cat that belonged to the lawyer
(according to the lawyer)
and who looked like the best conversation I was going to find.
I followed him behind the couch
and fell asleep.

all that poetry is

you see, is just
writing down what
it looks like
& sounds like
from the mind of a
two year old
child
reading life in any
which
way
other than the
way in which
it's written
feeding the fish
that swim
in
the heart
or jumping from
a rooftop
at sunset.

a beautiful day on Neptune

a catfish in
oven mitts tears
up the sun.

I was having sex
once while wearing a
ski suit when she said
what's taking so long?
and I told her *if you ever tried to pull
three inches out of 7,
you'd understand.*

but she didn't understand
and now we're divorced
(for other reasons, I hope.)

I watch from my second-floor
window as a red fox
darts across the two-lane,
stops and sits below
a streetlight.

the sun then moon then
stars then sun then moon
then stars again.

battleground

hate came so simple then
the power-struggle of
someday men in
the infant stages of
the schoolyard
bred
      through awkward eyes of
jealousy
 and indifference
the ugliness of
  upbringing
on display in
prey upon the weak
and less fortunate
getting your guts
     punched in
       for wearing cheap
            shoes
or moving about
awkwardly in the youth
 of bodies
trying to work it out
       with words that
      fell clumsily
  like darts
at the base of the
     board

we made our monsters there
amidst the cold sting of monkey-
bars and teeters of
        see-saws
— the invisible limits to
the four-squared world
  of our existence

like cubs in first freedom
facing conflict
we learned to fight the
  fight
when there was nowhere for
us to run
we fashioned our shells
against the world

that they've held up
as good
  as they have
still sometimes strikes with
surprise and
spreads a smile so rarely
displayed
during those many
     painful days
of making it.

a child tied to a roller coaster & hurled
into outer space

I wait inside my heart
like a small child
clinging to his mother's
skirt,

like a madman restrained in
a white & careful room,

like music in some
dusty old instrument..

I wait inside my heart
like fresh blood soaking
into a rug,

that you just let go on.

faster than the eye

the great stain left behind
a trick
a sleight of sight
great words by great men
like wine bleeding
into wood
a legacy left behind that
slowly loses its luster
one-by-one as the machines reach
termination & the world rolls over
spilling out from the tin
like colorful little monkeys
happy for a hole and the
mites that breed in their
fur

and what is best becomes what is easiest-
indifference in the 4th quarter of
the big one when the score gets
out of hand
flipping through the channels
trying to decide upon
which war to watch
while lying on your back
and lifting your legs
as the great vacuum of

corporation
sucks up the last of the crumbs
leaving us to squabble over
the shit
funneled into complacency
round up like cattle
with our pit-stains
and our neckties
eking out a living
some would call it
on our indigestion &
the blanketing calm of
our bureaucratic
prescriptions
as we are lured in
line by promise of
an open hand
as the blade sings
and the curtain
comes quietly
down.

chance

it is not chance
that we both stand at
5 and some odd inches
or that too much sun exposure is
certain to cause cancer

chance plays no part in good
conversation or the eventual death
of most anything, nor does it factor
into snake bites
or the lies of presidents

chance grows antsy sitting
on plush couch cushions
when shadows upon the walls
are still
& turns down dinner invites
when the guests are stiff-backed
and dull

it will never be identified by name
in the morning paper
you will only read about
its many exploits in the sporting
section, and even there its

presence is debatable
chance is what remains
when you put heat to
skill and effort—
I've done it many times
with mixed results

the act of banking on one
could be likened to
running for the swimming pool
during a hotel fire—

I would not recommend it.

a deduction of self

sitting amidst my ratty boxer shorts
on a chair in
the threshold between
the kitchen &
den, some poor dead bovine's skin
clinging tightly to my own
not yet dead
sweaty thighs

while someplace else
a black man sits in
a white house—

I happily helped put
him there;
call it the allure of change
or lethargy of war
either way,
our rattling bones of bigotry
are out of the closet now
and dancing to Jackie Wilson
tunes on the front lawn
while people flock to purchase shooters & steel
and fear for their money, values,
lives, yet they are already morally bankrupt,
devalued and eroding away
even more rapidly
than before.

I get up, dress, walk outside
point myself
towards the center of town
and begin walking..

soon staring at the dentist's office
I enter,
give them a name and
take a seat
as the waiting room begins
to throb all around me,
I am thinking in a Chinese accent
of the woman's legs behind the
counter and her beautiful heels
snug in her beautiful heels,
aching in my jaw and nostril
doggery of the air.

in and out of there in under an hour
roughly 3 grams lighter
and feeling a little less a piece of things
now as ever, lamenting the tiny parts of myself
but happy for the pain
only, I wish that that dentist
would have left the

rotten tooth and taken
the rest,

it might have been better
for the both of us.

action figure

she stands
stoically
in my bedroom
doorway—

a superhero
come to save me
from the cartoon villain
of myself.

inertia

I found an old rake
in the corner of
a garden;
handle rotted
away so that
only the teeth
were left.

I think I will lie
here
in this bed
for the next
50 years; through
two more world
wars, the colonization
of Mars & total death
of reality,

counting sun rises and
scratching in the
dirt until
they find
me.

natural cause

you would think he'd know
the way back out
through the window that
brought him in
but he seems confused
perplexed by the encasement of
these walls

now I find them to be
of comfort most often--
a bunker against the bomb
of humanity
but then again,
and it is unfortunate
for us both,
I can't fly away from trouble
in the way
that he has flown
into it

and now the cat is aware
and I am thinking he
must have been asleep
because his lack of response to
the commotion

has me doubting if he is really
the great hunter that
I think him to be
and the bird is now aware of
the cat too
as he flutters his wings
wildly
attempting the windows
at either end of the
narrow room

in nature, the bird is at great
advantage for escape and
yet will often times
fall victim to a seasoned
predator
but here
in this room
there is little space
for chance instead
only for the inevitability
of perpetual ending
as still silence of reward
and run of blood speaks
a truth—

there is no fair
no just anything
whether for the bird

the man or even
the cat
our untimely end shall
find us all—
a bright blade shining
in the night
or quiet consumption of cells

and as the sparrow meets his end
in the mouth of the cat
I think it the most honorable way for a bird
to go,

makes me almost wish
that I had feathers too.

they can't all be Picassos

sometimes
you just have to tell it
like it is,
drink it down
straight,

stare your enemy
in the eye,
kiss a girl half your age
on the mouth,
ring the bell
once for every fool
in the room

then get the hell
out of
there.

swarm of nothing
(for B. Tully)

waiting in line at the pump
for cheap fuel I have become
just another confused
bee of the swarm

attracted to the many shades of failure

waiting on the world to
come to me like
bucket for potato
peels,
and still the mouth goes hungry.

a car horn sounds 3 times
as an old man guides his Buick in,
yesterday's job is new again. I am
thankful for bridges made of steel
or these fingers being faulty
with flame.
the economy is in free-fall and yet
somehow
I have 2 jobs.
as I pull up to the pump,
put the car in park and think
of my friend,
now dead a week.

his body, a bone hotel in
a city of worms.
I think of the woman he left behind
and the bottomless sorrow of
those brown eyes.

they were to be married
she already had her dress,
a set date,
plans for children and
a new home.

I wipe a lone tear away as
the station attendant takes a
squeegee to my windshield.

you ought to be seeing clearly now, he says to me.
I thanked him anyhow
and drove away.

love

like matchsticks resilient
against the wind
burning
down to the
skin of
fingertips,

like stones
pressured against
one another until
they crumble in
two,

like a flapping reel
run out
when words
dry in the mouth

like worms
mixed up
in the sun.

Jesus save us all

empty fridge
& dreams of sirloin
warm beer
& no heat
huddled under a blanket
thinking of instant pudding
& timely love
as the cat tears at
the cork board
& plays with its fallen pieces
I've been doing much the same
with myself
making it work as
well as I can.
I think of love
and how it goes uneven—
when all the weight
slides hard to one side
like a fat kid on a
see-saw
waiting for
weightlessness.
I am dust
shot from a cannon
an empty spool of
heartstring

rolling across a
3 a.m. floor
waiting
for the neighbors
to hang up their
gloves, for a small
victory of some kind,
like notification of
an overpaid electric bill
or that the kitchen faucet
might stop dripping
but will instead ready
myself for the next great
disaster—
economic collapse and the inevitable water wars or
a Joel Osteen presidential
run.
I went to the doctor last
week and he told me
that I needed to cut back
on the sugar
and to stop
writing poems so late
in the evening,
he said all that burning
can't be good for your
heart.

laying on a Scottish hillside thinking about the masses and not much besides

laying upon this hill
overlooking the
ancient city
& the people don't
look so bad
really
going on about their day
as little paint speckles
flecked on
the great canvas of
the world.

like Uncle Milton's ants
down on the farm
they move
furiously this way
then that way—
I cover them over
with my thumb
but they keep crawling out
again and into
grocery stores
& cafes
museums and bus stations
offices of law

and commerce,
post and proctology,
into doors
around corners
and away from
my sight.

the traffic moves in a
collective hum
a tiny moped goes by
sounding like an
electric opener on
an old can of
spinach
but the ants themselves
are hushed
heads down and
determined
to reach their
destinations
much in the
same way that
I have been
in reaching mine
and from this very spot
it all looks quite harmless
and all the parts seem to work
well enough together
but then

even tragedies can
sometimes appear
beautiful
from a distance—
burning horses
running
from a burning barn

or

a bunch of weeds
twisted up
in the wind
like roses.

by the sea

it smells of salt
& everything is rusty
old pickups &
girls in colorful
barely anythings
& the breeze is more real
than a minute
an hour
an entire life
& love is good again
a shiny ring around the heart
that time can't have

the crab tastes wiser than his shell
and bug eyes might suggest
the beer brewed
with hints of old dreams

the dog shits the
sand sniffs awhile
then licks at sandy balls
and sleeps

the sun has pulled upon the
blanket of horizon
the skin plays pink

the people clear out and
finally peace
as the water beats against
a young child's
abandoned creation

the sun flies a kite of clouds
running with them
towards morning

while the sea
the pretty
poisonous sea
laps softly

waiting.

some get strong and some get strange

some get strong and some get
strange though I suppose the trick of it really
is maintaining one's endurance;
to do it right you have to conserve sanity for
the stretch run or risk a late-season breakdown—
the kind nobody comes back from.
I remember being 13 years old
and sitting in my friend Tim's mother's kitchen
as a line of cop cars sped by,
some kind of glowing
mad cavalry after an elderly woman took a
pot shot at us for walking past
her house on our way home
after school.
Old Lady Snavely we called her,
she was the dog that ate all the shit-house rats—
a truly deranged and demented sort, and on that day
she emerged from the house 4 feet and some odd
inches all bone
and villainy
when before we knew *what* a bullet came
whizzing our way... BAM!! sending me, my friend Tim
& my friend Other Tim scrambling for cover
as the shot missed our meat and hit something
immediately behind us. just then a
woman from across the street came,

all in hysterics screaming that she was calling the police,
as we ran and ran
from this 84 year old woman
as if she was hellfire, the devil incarnate,
we never did see her again after that
then a rumor was going around that the gun she fired
was made during the civil war and
worth a sizable fortune, and that the investigator was
surprised that it didn't explode in her hands as she fired.

I ran into Other Tim some several years back
outside of a Borders bookstore in our hometown,
he seemed to recognize me but looked right through me
in the kind of way that says *nothing*,
all glassy-eyed, wheel still spinning but the hamster's dead
kinda thing,
and the little bit that
was escaping his mouth made
even less sense still.

I had heard more recently that he was
working on the eighth floor of the Pentagon with top security
clearance, which kinda sounded like it was a way of saying
something else entirely but I hadn't
thought much
about that until just now.

remember—
it ain't a race.

success

I've trapped myself in with
a twelve pack, 18 jumbo eggs, loaf of bread,
worst case of heartburn, bag of smoke, two
days off and a passable excuse for
a third.

the ac is busted but the fan still works pretty good
and the Phillies have a day game
and the radio still plays
and I haven't vomited or
paid my taxes in nearly three years
which I know, sounds ridiculous.
I only even remember because the last time
it was my 26th birthday, Jack Daniels and
deer jerky and I drove home drunk
and yelled at my wife, threw things around,
then tore the covers from books
and vomited all over the bed.
I felt terrible and quite sorry
for being such the jerk but
what's there to do?

the past has this way of presenting itself
years later in a way
that leaves so little to interpretation

and I realize now
that everything has a pattern
and that some of those shirts
look better on the rack than
they ever will in the mirror
and I am nearly thirty
now, still no more a banker
than a bus driver,
no more a mailman than
anything at all

yet I smile
showing more teeth than I have in years—
there's no more deer jerky,
no more wife
but I can still hear the sun coming up
if I listen close and that's alright,
and every beer tastes like
a minor victory
and that's good too.

on my best days
I can look 25,
jog for miles and
be untouchable on a pool table,
hang picture frames
at 4 a.m. and
write the occasional
poem

and if that ain't success
then it is most likely I won't
ever really know
what is.

J. Lester Allen is an upstate NY poet who has scattered his work across the small press landscape having released three previous collections of work: *The Days Carnivore, Ask the Crows* and *A Cockroach in the Penthouse*. He can be reached at jlesterallen@gmail.com.

www.ingramcontent.com/pod-product-compliance
Lightning Source LLC
Chambersburg PA
CBHW030119100526
44591CB00009B/461